DEMYSTIFYING PROJECT MANAGEMENT

A Project Management Guide in Plain English for Startups

AHMED ZOUHAIR

"Don't let failure go to your heart, and don't let success go to your head."
—Will Smith

I believe that startups and entrepreneurs are at the core of any economy that is thriving. They are society's smartest and hardest workers. They also do more with fewer resources and support.

I want to dedicate this book to all of the startups and entrepreneurs, as well as to my grandfather, an entrepreneur who helped to create so many opportunities for his community. I hope this book will give y'all the confidence to launch or relaunch your businesses and be successful.

Thank you.

AHMED

CONTENTS

NOTE

How to Navigate This Book

This book is divided into four parts.

Part 1 explores the mission and purpose of your business. Why do you want to have a business? If you think of your business like a project, what goals and objectives surface?

Part 2 covers business strategy. What processes will you use to run your business? How can the Three Ps framework (Prepare, Plan, Perform) set you up for success?

Part 3 looks at project outcomes. What platforms, tools, and templates can help you achieve the desired result? In what ways might your project takeaways apply to future business applications?

Part 4 establishes your project team. Who will be doing the work? Why does division of labor matter, and how can it speed up the processes identified in Part 2?

INTRODUCTION

"Simplicity is the ultimate sophistication."
—Leonardo da Vinci

The Standish Group is a primary research advisory organization focusing on software development performance. Every two years, they publish the CHAOS Report, one of the most cited and globally recognized reports on IT project success rates and project management best practices. Each report is based on five years of data compiled from more than 50,000 in-depth project profiles. In 1994, the inaugural CHAOS Report showed that IT companies spend more than $140 billion on canceled and over-budget projects each year. The latest report—CHAOS2020: Beyond Infinity—categorized IT projects as Successful (delivered on time and on budget), Challenged (eventually delivered, but not on time or over budget), or Failed (nothing was delivered). The results were: Successful: 31%, Challenged: 50%, and Failed: 19%.

In short, the 2020 CHAOS Report concluded that the emerging criteria for project success were a good environment, a good team, and a good project sponsor. It went on to suggest that being agile and adaptable can lower project costs by a factor of four and

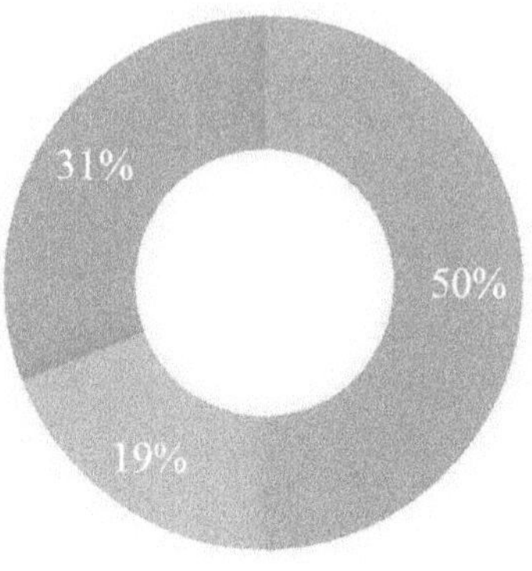

icrease the chances of success by 60% when compared to the traditional waterfall style of project management (wherein a project gets divided into distinct, sequential phases, with each new phase beginning only when the previous one has been completed).

That agility and adaptability can help a project succeed is important, since according to a report from the Bureau of Labor Statistics,[1] the majority of startups fail after two years in business. Half of those that fail do so due to poor operational planning and lack of project management application. An effective project management system (like the one described in this book!) can turn more Failed and Challenged businesses and projects into Successful businesses and projects, starting with a good environment, a good team, and a thoughtful project plan.

---

[1]   https://www.bls.gov/bdm/us_age_naics_00_table7.txt

PART 1
THE PURPOSE

Understanding Projects

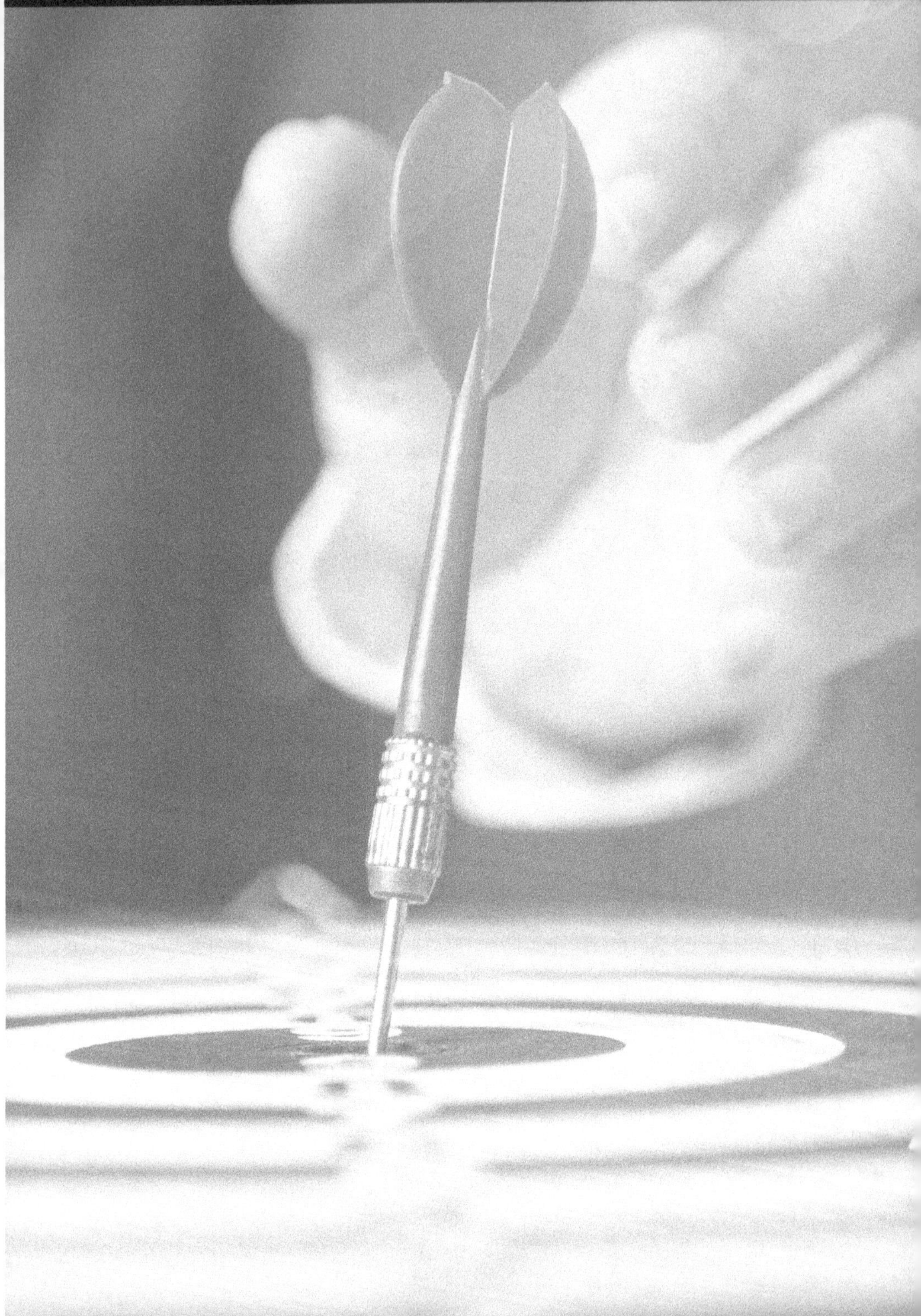

THE PURPOSE (WHY)

CHAPTER ONE

So, What Is a Project, Anyway?

In my experience, most entrepreneurs, including startup founders, are leaders and managers with passion, courage, resiliency, and the will to "get shit done" regardless of the challenges. They are natural-born project managers, even if they don't think of themselves that way or think that project management is too difficult. The misperception that project management must be complex stems, I believe, from the overuse of business jargon, mnemonics, acronyms, and other terminologies employed by some project management professionals.

For example, maybe you've heard, "A project is a problem scheduled for solution." Or, "All improvement takes place project-by-project and in no other way." Dr. Joseph M. Juran, widely regarded as the "founding father" of many of the quality management programs used by organizations today, once said that all projects should follow The Universal Sequence for Breakthrough. Mean anything to you? Me, either.

So, what is a project, anyway?

Allow me to offer you my favorite definition. More than just "a problem scheduled for solution," a project is *an opportunity scheduled for realization.* What this means is that every project has the potential to create meaning … especially in the world of the startup. Whether developing new products or services, preparing a response to a request for a proposal, adopting a new financial system, or creating a team to support a major new customer, almost every task undertaken by a startup can be reframed as a project—and further, as a chance to create meaning.

In the same way, project management is about capitalizing on that opportunity. While French mining engineer and business theorist Henri Fayol said that "to manage is to forecast and plan, to organize, to command, to coordinate and to control," it's more than that. Management might also require recruiting and training a project team, guiding and motivating that team, and doing the work alongside them. Project management more specifically takes into account the timeline and cost of a given project, as well as the resources available. It is the process of tracking the changes—the goals met—from a project's beginning to its end. For that reason, project management is considered both an art and a science. It is an art because it deals with intangible resources like people, and it is a science because it deals with tangible data using tools and processes.

The Information Overload

Most of us have been practicing project management all our lives without realizing it. Everything we do can be thought of like a project. Learning to read. Making the Little League team. Playing a musical instrument. Graduating college. Picking a mate. Becoming a good spouse. Finding and keeping a job. Maybe you've done some or all of the above. If so, good news: You've already developed an innate set of project management skills! Now it's time to refine them and apply them professionally, with intention, so you/your startup can be even more successful in this competitive world.

As a former project management training consultant and current small business owner, I have spent the last thirty years in the project management industry. During this time, I've worked for more than twenty organizations ranging from Fortune 500 companies (think Cisco and Thales) to smaller organizations such as Windstream and Transcomm. What I've found across the board is that the unique buzzwords, catchphrases, and acronyms each industry employs can be intimidating, overwhelming, or discouraging to those pursuing project management professions. Since there is no standardization of terminologies or tools among industries or even between competing companies, for a lot of project managers moving from one company to another is like learning another language. I decided to write this book to help those struggling with the information overload.

As the title advertises, *Demystifying Project Management: A Project Management Guide in Plain English for Startups* is just that. This book has been deliberately written in straightforward, jargon-free language understandable by anyone with even a modest background in business. It's designed to show you how to manage projects of all types, small or large, local or global, in-person or digital, for any kind of organization. I want it to be your toolbox—and I'm looking at you, engineers, software developers, managers, and teachers. Your toolbox is what you go to without thinking, knowing it has the thing you need, and knowing, too, where to find it. My hope is that it will lend structure to concepts you already know, show you how to apply those concepts properly, and serve as an ongoing reference book any time you're managing a project.

My "Why"

Although today I live and work in Austin, Texas, I actually was born and grew up in the country of Morocco. In 1988, I left for a better opportunity, and while I miss my hometown of Marrakesh, I've never looked back. Sometimes moving forward means leaving something else behind.

High-school-aged Ahmed was miserable. I was what you'd call a passive student, studying only for the purpose of passing exams without actually learning or retaining much at all. What little I did read was part of the school curriculum; if it wasn't assigned, you can bet I didn't read it. This was all well and good until, after graduating from a vocational training school in Casablanca with a certificate in Electronics, I couldn't find a job. Not only were there limited openings in that field at the time, but without the internet, I was dependent on word-of-mouth (and as you can imagine, my professional network was poor) or newspaper ads. Most of the jobs I saw advertised were for an intern technician position fixing electronics equipment like televisions, radios, and stereos. Nothing wrong with that—except, for the first time in my life, I wanted more.

"More" eventually took the form of a job interview with Phillips Petroleum. I'll never forget how badly the interview went. It was with a French guy maybe named Phillips as well. He asked a lot of technical questions I wasn't prepared to answer, seeing as there were no "interview prep" resources back then. Also, although I looked presentable, I didn't look professional. I was too nervous to even speak properly. It should come as no surprise, then, that I did not get the job.

Nevertheless, the interview and the opportunity it promised inspired me. After exhausting all my options at home, in 1988 I moved to the US to continue my studies in Electrical Engineering. I showed up at the University of Texas-Austin with an international student visa and a renewed commitment to making something of my life. It would become my "why," the reason I've worked as hard as I have since then. I wanted to nail every job interview

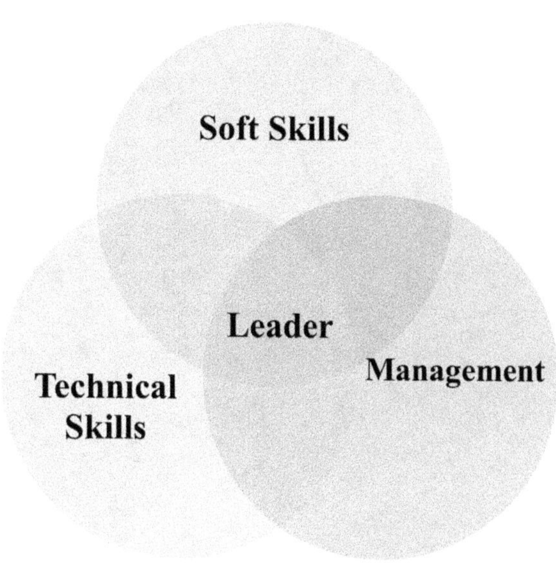

thereafter, so I could become a leader who helps others like me.

After nailing many job interviews and learning from some of the top leaders in their fields, what I now know about leadership is this: Successful leaders have great soft skills, technical skills, and management skills, in addition to being adaptable and being great communicators. They understand how to align people, tools, and processes toward the end of running faster, better, and more efficient businesses. In other words, they are excellent project managers.

Getting Certified

How can *you* become an excellent leader and project manager? Does it mean obtaining more certifications and adding more letters after your name? Not necessarily! While hard work and train-

#TOOMANYCERTIFICATIONS

ing never hurt anyone, there's always more time to improve your credentials. An alternative, yet equally effective, approach to just signing up for every program under the sun is to start by determining which organizations you'd like to work for as a project manager. Each organization has its own requirements. Some may want you to have the PMP (Project Management Professional), CSM (Certified ScrumMaster), and/or ITIL (Information Technology Infrastructure Library) certifications, while others don't place as much importance on those letters. It's also worth pointing out here that the credentials alone don't make someone a qualified project manager! For that reason, I would highly recommend focusing first on getting as much experience in project management as possible prior to pursuing any certifications. See demystifyingproject-management.com for a list of ways to gain experience without credentials.

When you do decide it's time to pursue certification, you'll want to prepare appropriately. In a nutshell, getting ready to take the PMP exam or any other certification test is similar to taking the SAT, GRE, or GMAT. There are classes you can take to help you learn the right material, which you'll need to pass the exam—and then likely never need again. So much of what I call book-learning is regurgitated theories and facts. It gets you the letters after your name, which in turn can get you a job, but it's always better if, from the beginning, you attempt to apply whatever you're learning to real-world situations based on your personal experience. The material will make more sense to you, you'll retain it longer, and you'll also be more relaxed and more successful on Test Day.

With all of that in mind, are you ready to tackle your first project—i.e. your own startup? In the next chapter, we'll look at when it makes sense to view your business like a project, why doing so can help you work smarter, not harder, and how this method can keep you from joining the 50% of startups that fail in their first two years.

VISION, MISSION, GOALS

CHAPTER TWO

Project Vision, Mission, Goals, and Guiding Principles

"A vision on its own is not enough. Hard work and dedication is required to make that vision a reality."
—Strive Masiyiwa, Econet Wireless

"To build a successful business, you must start small and dream big. In the journey of entrepreneurship, tenacity of purpose is supreme."
—Aliko Dangote, Dangote Group

Small or large, your business can be treated like a project. As with any other project, your business (regardless of industry) has requirements, a timeline, quality standards, and a budget. The products or services your business sells are steps along the way to meeting your project's goal: usually, generating a profit by satisfying your customers' needs. To that end, there are four essential tools we can talk about to help you conceive of your business like a project. They are vision, mission, goals, and guiding principles—and they are the cornerstones of business success.

Among small business owners and entrepreneurs, these four words can cause confusion. Anything we don't understand can be intimidating! However, there is no reason to fear them; just the opposite, as your vision, mission, goals, and guiding principles serve to identify why you are in business, what you want to achieve, and how you will get there. In addition, they can help you define and describe how your business operates and/or differs from your competition.

Too many business owners don't take the time to develop their vision, mission, goals, and guiding principles. They don't understand that planning the direction of their business is as important as the product or service they offer. If they do take the time, they tend to keep the results to themselves, never sharing them with their employees and customers. They miss out on a great opportunity to connect with their target audience, and as a result, many entrepreneurs don't achieve the success they seek. Like the late great baseball player, manager, and coach Yogi Berra said: They

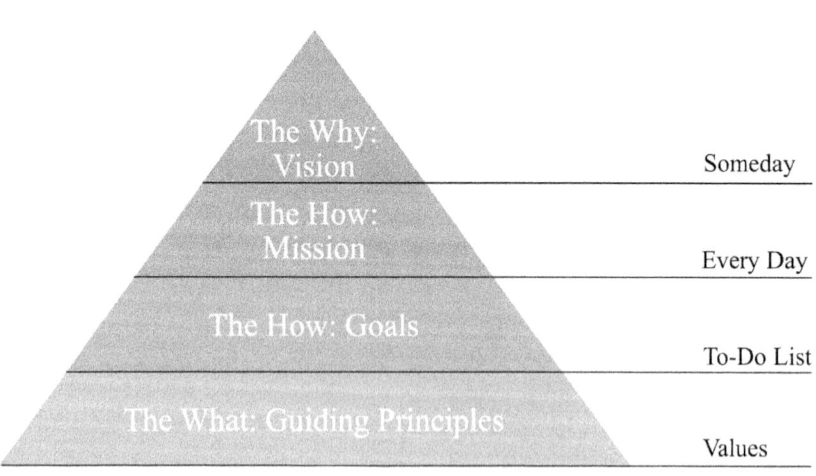

don't know where they are going, so they never get there.

You, on the other hand, want to get there. I know you do; why else would you be reading this book? Without further ado, let's dive in. By the end of this chapter, you will have a clear understanding of vision, mission, goals, and guiding principles, and how to apply them to your business-cum-project.

Vision

Vision is how you define success in business in the long-term—anywhere from five to 100 years. To determine your vision, try answering the simple question, "Why are we here, and where are we going as a business?" Your vision is what propels your business into the future. A grand vision inspires and motivates everyone involved and sets you apart from the competition.

A good example of a successful startup with a strong vision is iManila, a marketing and branding company in the Philippines. iManila's vision, as stated on the company's website, is "to optimize and simplify customer journeys." The way iManila achieves that vision is through its mission (more on missions in a minute): "to provide exceptional IT, web, and digital solutions to clients in the hopes of improving their lives." The startup was founded by two brothers in 1996 with an investment of $1,253—and has since grown to 58 employees and $11 million in sales as a result of iManila's clear focus on its vision, mission, and overall business strategy.

Your vision statement should express your core ideology and values. It explains why you exist and what you stand for. At iManila, a vision of optimizing and simplifying customer journeys reflects that company's commitment to putting people first. It underpins everything they do, and because it's a core value, it's not about to change anytime soon. This aspect is crucial, because as best-selling business author Jim Collins states, your vision statement should pass the test of time. It should not be limited to what's trending, but hold up far into the future.

In his book *The Infinite Game*, inspirational speaker Simon Sinek compares a well-written vision statement to "a just cause." When people believe in a cause strongly enough, they will do whatever it takes to make it happen. If you can get your employees to buy in to your company's vision with a similar fervor, they'll naturally show up and work hard for you every day. (A survey conducted by Dynamic Signal in 2017 revealed that employees who feel inspired by their employer's vision statement are 18% more productive.[1])

Sinek goes on to advise that your vision should be inclusive, resilient, and service-oriented. "Inclusive" means it is open to anyone who wants to help achieve the vision and does not leave anyone out. "Resilient" means your vision will be able to survive technological and cultural changes, or at least be able to recover and respond quickly. "Service-oriented" means that the focus of the vision is on the stakeholders—your customers, investors, employees, and partners. The best vision statements focus more on the communities you want to serve than on your business itself.

American online shoe and clothing retailer Zappos is another example of a business with a customer-focused, timeless, and values-driven vision statement. Originally, the company's branding was all about having the best online collection of shoes and clothes, but later on, CEO Tony Hsieh switched Zappos's "reason for being" to providing the best customer service. They created a four-pronged approach to, as they describe it, "delivering happiness," centered on the four Cs of commerce, customer service,

---

1   https://dynamicsignal.com/2017/04/21/employee-productivity-statistics-every-stat-need-know/

company culture, and community. What this looks like in practice is a vast selection of products with good quality and design, 24/7 customer service, free shipping, free returns, VIP membership, a library for employees, and complimentary rides from the airport for employees. Zappos grew so large that Amazon acquired it in 2009 for $1.2 billion.

Finally, there's Waze, the driving directions app. Though it has stiff competition from Google Maps, Waze has a more dedicated user base due to its comprehensive GPS navigation system that gives drivers real-time traffic reports along with estimated travel times and recommended route details. Waze's vision is to "improve the quality of everyone's daily driving"—something anyone who's ever driven can get behind, no?

In summary: A clear and compelling vision converts clients, encourages and motivates employees, and reminds you why you got into business in the first place.

Vision Case Study, or Why I Got into Business in the First Place

Every time an adult asks a kid what they want to be when they grow up, that kid answers with their personal vision statement.

"I want to be a firefighter and save people's lives."

"I want to be president of the United States and save the planet."

"I want to be a police officer and get the bad guys."

It's crystal clear, values-driven, and timeless.

When I was a kid, my answer sounded like, "I want to be a business owner, just like my grandfather." As the greatest man I knew,

he inspired the sum total of my vision.

Haj Tahar Zouhair left his home in rural Morocco and walked 200 miles to the city of Marrakesh when he was still a teenager. He brought the harvest from his family's farm on ten camels and sold it in the farmers' market. With the proceeds, he started trading in other produce such as eggs, flour, and sugar. Eventually, he added trucking to his business and began shipping and receiving goods all over the country. Haj grew his business until it had more than 100 drivers, 40 trucks, and multiple warehouses staffed by employees. He never worked for anyone and loved being an entrepreneur long before that word became popular. I admired him greatly, as did my father and brothers, who followed in his footsteps and run my grandfather's business to this day.

As I kid, I thought the best part of my grandfather's work was that any time he traveled to Spain, he brought home candy and toys for the kids. Oh, to have money and be able to buy whatever I liked! As I got older, however, I realized the larger benefits of working for oneself—things like setting my own schedule, having time off to spend with my family, and creating jobs for other people in the community. Over the years, my vision changed from merely being a business owner to helping to improve people's lives.

After I emigrated to the US (and learned English and saved enough money working two jobs at Kentucky Fried Chicken and as a math tutor to pay tuition at UT-Austin), I entered the American job market with a purpose. I wanted to make sure that I worked for a company with a good vision, mission, goals, and guiding principles. When multinational technology corporation IBM offered me a summer internship, I took it gladly, proud not only to be joining the world's most successful information technology company, but one with a great vision: to improve business, society, and the human condition through the application of intelligence, reason, and science. Sure enough, I gained valuable experience in leadership, networking, and professional development at IBM.

I then spent the next twenty years as a consultant in project management and engineering while getting a master's in Management Information Systems from UT-Dallas and a doctorate in Business Administration from the University of the Incarnate Word. Despite all my education and experience, when I started my first company in 2006, I failed to establish a vision for my business, which was a project management training and consulting firm. Lacking an overriding purpose, clear structure, or tangible goals, my business never took off. I could not generate a continuous stream of income or grow until I revisited these business cornerstones.

Because the vision statement I settled on—to improve people's lives—is both timeless and customer-focused, I was able to weather the seismic shifts in the technology sector when FAANG (Facebook, Apple, Amazon, Netflix, and Google) appeared on-scene almost fifteen years ago. These platform giants have forced a lot of small businesses to shutter their doors, and many more to change their business strategies. I deviated slightly away from providing direct project management services to focus more on coaching, training, and speaking. Today, I help people both personally and professionally by finding them business opportunities where resources are scarce. This industry requires flexibility. You have to pivot to where business opportunities are available. It requires being innovative and creative, and being unafraid to challenge the status quo by taking calculated risks and having a mindset of fearless entrepreneurial leadership. In many ways, what I do today is much like what my grandfather did sixty years ago—only without the camels!

Mission

Think of the mission statement like the action plan for the vision statement. You've outlined what's important to you/your business; now how are you going to make it happen? Like your vision statement, your mission statement for your business should be simple, straightforward, objective, and realistic. Most of all, it should be concise: 140 to 280 characters (like a tweet!) is the sweet spot. The style should fit the audience for which it is intended. A mission statement developed for bankers or educators may be more formal, whereas a mission statement meant to guide a high tech company can be much more informal.

The mission statement for my coaching business is "to quietly inspire and help people reach their full potential." I'll save you from counting and just tell you that statement has exactly fifty-two characters. I spent a lot of time thinking about it, making sure that it fits my beliefs and purpose. It covers all that I want to do, including coaching, consulting, speaking, and giving training workshops. It also dovetails perfectly with my vision of improving people's lives.

Overall, a mission statement is meant to guide day-to-day operations while helping a company plan for the future. It's possible to arrive at a mission statement that is too broad or non-specific, and therefore meaningless when it comes to serving as a company's North Star. The mission statement of the LaTex Project Public License (LPPL), for example, is: "To satisfy our customers' desires for personal entertainment and information through total customer satisfaction." I'll admit, I've read it ten times and I still don't know what this mission statement means. What is "personal entertainment"? Could they have picked a broader category than "information"? I don't think so. And how exactly do they plan to achieve total customer satisfaction?

These companies' mission statements aren't much better:

- Hatton National Bank: "Combining an entrepreneurial spirit with empowered people and leading-edge technology to constantly exceed stakeholder expectations." (Too broad.)
- ADITYA: "To supply outstanding service and solutions through dedication and excellence." (Reads too much like a statement of core values.)

In *The Mission Statement Book: 301 Corporate Mission Statements from America's Top Companies*, Jeffrey Abrahams recommends that when writing a mission statement, you avoid commonly overused words as they don't create an impact anymore. He cites some of the terms most frequently used by mission statement writers (see table below), and suggests you avoid them when possible, or use them sparingly if you must.

If a vision statement declares what you do and why, the mission statement explains how you will do it. A well-designed mission statement helps you navigate your way through any kind of prob-

Word	Frequency of use
service	230
customers	211
quality	194
value	183
employees	157
growth	118
environment	117
profit	114
shareholders	114
leader	104
best	102

lem, roadblock, or other difficulty you encounter. So long as your mission is clear and you stick to it, you will get where you want to be!

Everyone enjoys picking on Amazon these days because they have become enormously successful. Many forget that Amazon was founded in 1994 and did not become profitable until the fourth quarter of 2001. Even then, their profits were just $5 million on a revenue of more than $1 billion. Despite seven years of struggling to turn a profit, they stuck to their mission, and in the first quarter of 2021, reported $108 billion in revenue with earnings of $8 billion. Today they are the most successful company on the planet.

In my current business, my mission is to take action now and every day to become an inspiring and quiet leader, and profitable business coach, speaker, and trainer. It's how I help my clients improve their personal and professional lives. When creating your mission statement, think about inspiring your stakeholders and grabbing the attention of prospects through word-of-mouth. Satisfied clients, old and new, become the tribe that will support your business and help you grow.

In his book *Start with Why*, Simon Sinek states, "People don't buy what you do; they buy why you do it. And what you do simply proves what you believe." A perfect example of this philosophy is the success of Tesla, the first fully electric car to reach worldwide public acceptance. Its customers are not just buying a car; they're buying into the cause of green energy. With every purchase, they're supporting climate change initiatives and easing pollution caused by fossil fuels. In other words, they love Tesla's vision. If Tesla did not follow through with an equally worthy mission, though—backing up their vision with good design, reliable technological gadgets, and a quirky CEO—their "how"—customers would look elsewhere for a product that had a similar vision but a better mission.

Goals

Goals are the tangible activities needed to achieve the vision and mission. They are, in layman's terms, your to-do list.

I have set some ambitious goals for myself in the coming year, including:

Professional goals
- Conduct 50 paid speeches worldwide
- Coach 50 customers
- Conduct 25 workshops in entrepreneurship, management, and technology
- Consult part-time for 15 hours a week

Personal goals

- Provide five free workshops a year to some of my favorite associations, charities, and non-profits
- Practice yoga three times a week and play soccer once a week
- Write one book
- Listen to 50 podcasts
- Read at least 15 books
- Do a TEDx talk
- Take guitar and voice lessons
- Visit three new countries
- Volunteer for at least 5 hours a month

By tackling these goals, I will achieve my mission of helping people reach their full potential as well as my vision of improving people's lives.

What goals come to mind immediately for your business?

Guiding Principles

According to the Oxford Dictionary, guiding principles are "standards of behavior; one's judgment of what is important in life." They are a unique set of moral, non-negotiable values that drive your business behavior and decision-making. Guiding principles create a social environment much like a tribe, attracting like-minded employees. They form a healthy company culture where everyone understands what matters most.

Guiding principles overlap with our social and business responsibilities. They may include such values as being compassionate, courageous, or honest. Guiding principles are different from those values shaping your vision statement because they are, first and foremost, meant to keep people in line. There will be consequences if anyone, regardless of their rank in the industry, breaks these principles.

I recommend that all small business owners have their employees come up with their own guiding principles. The process doesn't take long and can pay enormous dividends, as working on this task together creates a sense of partnership and responsibility to the company. Set up a two-hour workshop and have the employees list those values that matter most to them. What are the non-negotiable principles that guide them? Let the list emerge organically through collaboration, and then prioritize it.

By way of example, my business's guiding principles look like this:

- compassion
- cooperation
- collaboration
- trustworthiness
- honesty with my clients and team

A few hours of brainstorming can make all the difference in creating shared principles that will carry the company far into the future.

As a business grows, its goals may change, but its guiding principles should remain the same. They are the values that matter most to your business. Occasionally, you may add to the principles, much the way we change the United States constitution. Today, companies might want to foster an inclusive, diverse workplace and zero tolerance for sexual harassment.

Putting It All Together: Why Do Vision, Mission, Goals, and Guiding Principles Matter?

Suppose you are the sole employee of your business or that you have only a few employees. You may think you can't spare the time to create a solid foundation for your business. You are too busy working night and day to get it started! You may tell yourself

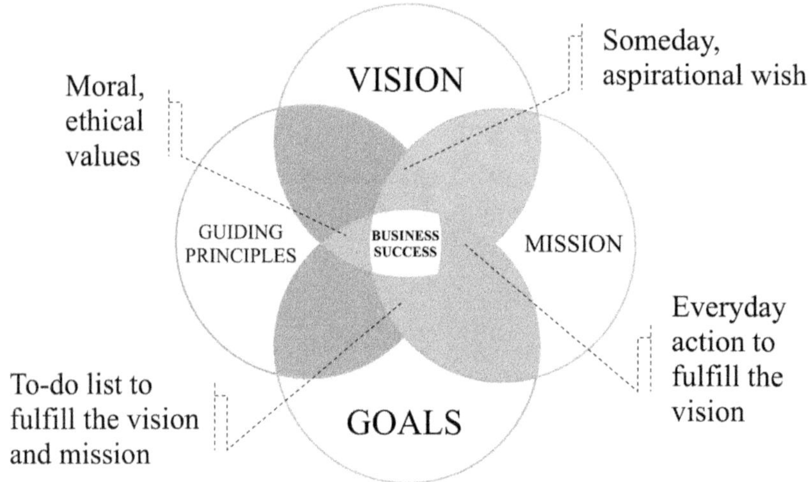

that determining a clear vision, mission, goals, and guiding principles is a waste of time. After all, aren't they just words that big companies put on plaques they hang on the wall?

Nothing could be further from the truth. One of the reasons some companies become more prominent and successful than others is the clarity of their purpose. If the employees understand and support the vision, mission, goals, and guiding principles, the organization is far more likely to be successful.

Remember: The vision is the aspirational, inspirational, long-term plan for your business. The mission includes the day-to-day operations that will fulfill the vision. Goals are the tangible to-do list of tasks needed to achieve the vision and mission. Guiding principles are a set of non-negotiable morals and timeless values that inform business conduct and decision-making. Each one plays a vital role in the success of your business. If you put in the time and effort to create these cornerstones with input from your team, this groundwork will help prepare you for your business's growth and whatever changes or challenges it may face. They will steer you down the right path where you will find your passion and purpose.

Part 1 Workbook: Examples of VMG&GP (Vision, Mission, Goals, and Guiding Principles) by Industry

Below, I have provided some examples of small businesses and startups in developing countries. These companies face particular struggles, like a lack of resources (finances, technology, and infrastructure) and support, that companies in developed nations do not—so they are worth including for that perspective alone.

Name & Country	Vision	Mission
Tpaga Financial Services, Colombia	To shape the future of payments	To help customers make any type of disbursement or transfer without using banks
Bookdoc Health & Wellness, Malaysia	Bridging behavioral and physical health to create a happier and healthier world	To deliver to patients effective mental health care

Name & Country	Goals	Guiding Principles
Tpaga Financial Services, Colombia	Improve payment experience; increase operational efficiency; minimize cash handling	Immediacy Loyalty Cost control
Bookdoc Health & Wellness, Malaysia	Simplify patient care for professionals; help hospitals scale and increase performance; make the consultation process easier	Connect Empower Achieve

Application

What is the VMG&GP for your business? It's okay if you don't have a business yet. Maybe you're thinking about starting one. This is a perfect time to consider your VMG&GP. If you do already have a business but never took the time to create this vital blueprint, dive in! This is your chance to take what we've been discussing and put it into practice. What follows is one example of what your VMG&GP might look like. Remember, concision is key and less is more.

VMG&GP	Statements
Vision	
Mission	
Goals	
Guiding Principles	

See more examples of good vision and mission statements on the next page.

Companies with a Good Vision Statement

Name	Vision Statement
IKEA	To create a better everyday life for many people
Nike	To bring inspiration and innovation to every athlete
Oxfam	To create a world without poverty
Southwest	To be the world's most loved, most efficient, and most profitable airline
Ted	To spread ideas

Companies with a Good Mission Statement

Name	Mission Statement
Patagonia	To build the best product, cause no unnecessary harm, use business to inspire, and implement solutions to the environmental crisis
Honest Tea	To create and promote great-tasting, healthy, organic beverages
Nordstrom	To give customers the most compelling shopping experience possible
Prezi	To reinvent how people share knowledge, tell stories, and inspire their audiences to act
Twitter	To give everyone the power to create and share ideas and information instantly, without barriers

THE PROCESS (HOW)

PART 2
THE PROCESS

Launching or Relaunching a Project

STRATEGY

CHAPTER THREE

Project Strategy

"Business is always a struggle. There are always obstacles and competitors. There is never an open road, except the wide road that leads to failure. Every great success has always been achieved by fight. Every winner has scars. The men who succeed are the efficient few—they are the few who have the ambition and willpower to develop themselves. So, choose to be among the few today."
—Chris Kirubi, Centum Investment

"Action without vision is only passing time, vision without action is merely daydreaming, but vision with action can change the world."
–Nelson Mandela

Now let's look at the development, design, and implementation of your business strategy. Strategy is a process that begins when you found your business, takes you to market, and sees you through to your first customer and beyond. It's not enough to *have* a strategy; you have to implement it, too.

The Well-Crafted Strategy

Once you've developed your business goals (see Chapter Two for a refresher on goals at any point), the next step is to determine the best strategy to achieve them. A strategy is a set of clear, tangible, and specific measures that must be taken to reach your goals. For example, if I am serious about doing fifty paid speaking engagements in the current fiscal year, then I must undertake a number of actions to make that happen. Talking about it or dreaming about it won't get it done. As author Rick Page said, "Hope is not a strategy." Strategy is an action verb. It is the opposite of wishful thinking.

A goal of growing your business might involve a strategy of reaching out to new market segments. Alternatively, it might mean developing new products and services, or strategically changing your pricing. Businesses must select the most appropriate strategies for their goals that also align with their business vision, mission, and guiding principles.

For any strategy to work, you must be disciplined and laser-focused. It's all too easy for business owners to get sidetracked or distracted by other opportunities that are not relevant to their goals. You may be offered a chance to be president of your local Rotary Club, or be invited to consult for a company as a contractor where you will make a lot of money over a long period of time. While these are tempting opportunities, you may have to turn them down if accepting them will prevent you from achieving your goals. You have to stay on task to get them done.

The same is true in your personal life. Let's say one of your well-to-do clients invites you for an all-expenses-paid vacation sailing on their new yacht. It sounds like the trip of a lifetime, but it will take you away from your business for a month. If you're serious about what you say you want to accomplish, you will thank them and politely decline. Your priorities must come first.

A successful business strategy focuses as much on the customer as it does on any potential business profit. It creates a lasting relationship based on trust and commitment to the customers' interests. If I'm writing a speech as part of meeting my goal of giving fifty paid speeches, the focus of said speech must be on giving the audience techniques or ideas that will help them be more successful. It must be full of useful, value-added content—useful for the audience, not for me. If my speech is successful in connecting with the audience and inspiring them, then I am successful. I'd rather receive a silent ovation for making a real difference than a standing ovation for a speech that whips my audience into a frenzy but leaves them with no meaningful takeaways.

The Why, How, and What of Strategy

To determine the best strategy for achieving your specific goals, remind yourself of your purpose. Why did you go into business? Then, link your purpose to your process. How will you make your vision and mission a reality?

A well-crafted strategy is what inspires the small business owner to get out of bed every morning, rain or shine, and do the work that needs to be done. It is indeed what motivates, inspires, and keeps them going. Don't believe me? Here's a story.

A medieval traveler is wandering around the country and comes across a vast construction project. Along his path, he sees three bricklayers, hard at work.

"What are you doing?" he asks.

The first worker says, "I'm building a wall."

The second bricklayer responds,"I'm laying bricks to feed my family."

The third bricklayer, with a smile on his face, announces, "I'm building a great cathedral to the Almighty."

We can't know if there is any difference in the skill level of these workers, but they vary greatly in how they see themselves and their purpose. The first bricklayer is hyper-focused on the task at hand. The second and third see themselves as part of something bigger (a family or all of creation), but only the third conceives of himself as an integral part of a great project that will last for hundreds of years to come. The third bricklayer is most keenly aware of his "why."

But what about the "how"?

Like the bricklayer who must refine his craft to a degree worthy of the Almighty, if I'm serious about booking paid speeches, I have to develop a strategy, too. First I have to write the speech. Then I must rehearse it, deliver it in front of friendly audiences, and make changes based on feedback. Next, I must market the speech on my website and social media to current and previous clients and in networking groups. I need to let people know that I'm ready for business. I may have to give the speech for free several times to get the word out and practice. I might use this book or a workshop as a way of promoting my speaking and business coaching. If I spend the time, energy, and money to take all of those specific actions, then I have a real shot at achieving my goal.

As for the "what" of business strategy … well, that's the outcome you hope to achieve by reaching your goal. If you don't know what it is by now, return to the Part 1 Workbook and revisit your goals. Reading ahead won't do you any good until you do. If, on the other hand, you have clear goals, and you know your why, how, and what, keep reading to learn how to maximize your strategy's chances of success.

Differentiation

A strong strategy can set you apart from the crowd, helping to differentiate you from your competitors. According to Dr. Michael Porter, one of the gurus of economics and business strategy, differentiation happens when you create a unique product or offer a service no one else does. You can also differentiate by creating something difficult to copy. Spotify streams free music to 500 million listeners around the globe. The platform personalizes the music it delivers to listeners based on their own preferences, as captured by a proprietary algorithm. There is no comparable company with Spotify's customer base and loyalty. It was the first of its kind in this space, and remains the leader in its category.

As part of your strategy, ask yourself: How can you differentiate your product or service?

Cost Leadership

Cost leadership is when business owners create economies of scale through highly efficient operations that produce goods and services for a lower cost or even for free.

Zoom is a perfect example of the explosive growth that can take place when a product meets a pressing need in the marketplace. Zoom went from 10 million users at the end of 2019 to 300 million by March of 2021—an increase of 2,900%—by offering their online teleconferencing software for free to schools and universities during the COVID-19 lockdown. Today, the word "Zoom" has become a verb just like Google.

Is there room in your business strategy for your company to be-

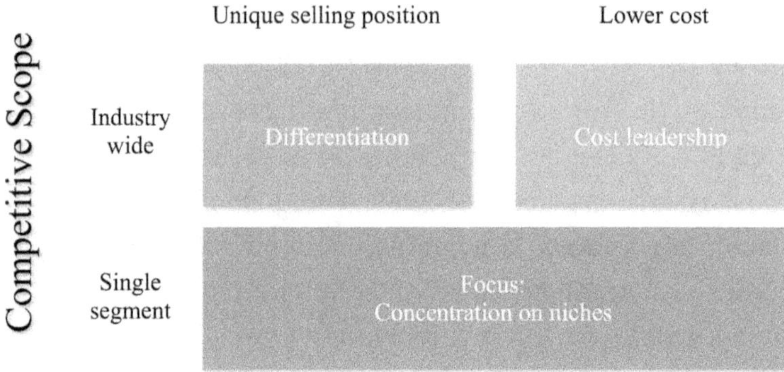

come a cost leader in some way, even if only in the short-term?

Segmentation

Segmentation occurs when you create a niche market.

Messaging app Slack bills itself as "the collaboration hub that brings the right people, information, and tools together to get work done," and is a perfect example of segmenting in the marketplace. Slack is an easy-to-use-and-administer application that facilitates online communication among teams within organizations. By allowing companies to replace internal emails, text messages, and/or instant messages with one streamlined communication channel, it met a clear need, and between 2014 and 2020, amassed 12 million users while competing with Microsoft and Apple.

Tesla likewise segmented the automobile industry when on August 2, 2006, Elon Musk announced Tesla's strategic plan. It was:

- Build and sell sports car at $130,000.
- Use the profits to build and sell an affordable car at $75,000.
- Use those profits to build and sell an even more affordable car at $33,000.
- While doing all of the above, provide zero-emission electric power generation.

Does your business operate in an industry ripe for segmentation?

When Strategies Fail

Not all strategies are created equal. Even those that draw on differentiation, cost leadership, and/or segmentation can sometimes fail.

I once worked for a company that offered billing platforms for telecom and cable companies. Our sales team then sold the platform to a non-telecom company, requiring us to customize it. We basically had to re-develop the entire platform, tweaking it to fit the new customer's requirements and testing its functionality in that capacity. It soon became apparent that the sales team had sold an offering we couldn't support. The company's leadership was stubborn, however, and determined to deliver the service to make a profit. They directed the worker bees—me included—to keep trying to make it work. The project was put on hold three times. Ultimately, it was canceled because we sold something we couldn't make or support.

Reader, beware when planning your strategy: Are you making promises you won't be able to keep?

Putting It All Together: Your Game Plan

The bottom line in business is that you must have a game plan—a strategy—to be successful. Your strategy should align at all times with your business's vision, mission, and guiding principles.

To determine your strategy, start with your goals. Where do you want to be? What is the ideal end state for your product or service? Figure that out, then work backward from there. Along the way, consider whether it makes sense to differentiate yourself, act as a cost leader, or segment the market in some way. If it does and you can, you're more likely to come up with a winning, not a failing, strategy.

Part 2a Workbook: The SWOT Analysis

One more tool can help make sure you're developing a foolproof strategy to meet your business goals. The SWOT analysis will help you identify, so you can address, your business's strengths, weaknesses, opportunities, and threats.

STRENGTHS	I N T E R N A L	WEAKNESSES
•Strength #1 •Strength #2		•Weakness #1 •Weakness #2
OPPORTUNITIES	E X T E R N A L	THREATS
•Opportunity #1 •Opportunity #2		•Threat #1 •Threat #2

PREPARE

CHAPTER FOUR

Project Preparation

"Focus on making your product or service awesome. I see a lot of guys go into business with a 'how can I make money' approach. But if you go in there saying 'how can I make something awesome,' the money will follow."
—*Alex Fourie, iFix*

"I am guided each day by these three questions: 'What are you fixing?' 'What are you making?' and 'Who are you helping?'"
—*Juliana Rotich, Ushahidi*

In this chapter, we will be addressing pre-planning, or the preparation that goes into setting up a project or business prior to kickoff. Preparation or pre-planning is the first P in the 3Ps approach to the project lifecycle.

The 3Ps Approach
- Preparing
- Planning
- Performing

THE 3Ps APPROACH

Prepare	Plan	Perform
• Problem defintion	• Priorities	• Shipping
• Requirements	• Work	• Customer service
• Contract and RFP	• Budget	• Tracking
• Resources	• Timeline	• Lessons learned
• Tools	• Team	

Each P is important and we will study each in turn. For now, just know that in addition to the preparation methodologies that follow, there are logistical considerations like establishing charters, stakeholder registers, contracts and other templates that exceed the scope of this book. For more information on these parts of preparation, see www.demystifyingprojectmanagement.com

The 50%

Have you ever wondered why half of all businesses fail in the first two years? For most of them, they've failed even before getting started.

In today's very competitive environment, making a business succeed is not only about determination and problem-solving. There is a very important aspect that startups often neglect, but which is critical to the success of any project. It's pre-planning/preparation.

Most entrepreneurs grow their business by getting things done as fast as possible. They're generally pressured by market changes, customers, and competition. They may think that fast execution is the most efficient way and that they cannot afford to lose time to preparation.

The truth is that pre-planning saves you a lot of time regardless of the pressure, tension, deadlines, budget, and other business constraints. The results of poor preparation can be very devastating to any business.

All we have to do is look at the COVID-19 pandemic. It surprised the world. No country was prepared for it, and as a result, we all suffered the consequences. Some countries adapted better than others, but the losses endured were so significant that many people and businesses may never recover from them.

It's not just pandemics, either. Natural disasters like fires, flooding, and hurricanes also tend to catch us off-guard, and their damage can be extraordinary. So can the damage caused by everyday unforeseen circumstances. The solution? Become better prepared.

Preparation saves you the time and resources that would otherwise be consumed by solving unexpected problems. It's the best way to avoid the negative consequences of bad surprises and be ready to face almost any situation.

Understanding Preparation

In its most basic sense, preparation means doing your homework. What preparation entails will look different depending on the specific application. You might "prepare" for any of the following to some degree:

a) a job interview
b) exam preparation
c) going on a trip
d) buying a house
e) getting married/divorced
f) leaving a legacy
g) having children/parenting.

Pick one of the events above, and ask yourself: What kind of preparation would help you succeed?

Preparation and Personal Experience

Now, pick an experience from your own life that you know requires preparation—and try to answer the questions below:

- What would happen if you didn't prepare? Or half-prepared?
- Do you feel like you have enough time to prepare?
- How do you know when you are fully prepared?
- What motivates/inspires/pushes/encourages you to prepare?
- What is your definition of preparation?

How you answer these questions will reveal your current approach to preparation/pre-planning. Are you ready to incorporate it fully and succeed?

Forms of Preparation

As just illustrated, preparation may take different forms depending on the situation. The end result, however, should always be the same. Preparation is all about getting things done in the most effective and efficient way.

Synonyms for preparation include, but are not limited to:

- requirements
- checklist
- steps (step-by-step instructions)
- to-do list
- activities
- communication plan
- tasks
- milestones
- deliverables
- plan
- roadmap
- game plan
- schedule
- risks
- concerns
- lessons learned

Whatever term you prefer, on the next page is a template for a to-do list table to help you organize all your tasks and keep track of your progress.

Eisenhower Matrix

Aside from to-do lists, the Eisenhower Matrix is another useful tool for managing your daily tasks and focusing on what will make you not only productive, but effective. It helps you to organize your tasks according to importance and urgency. All of your daily tasks, no matter how big or small, fall into one of these four categories:

- Urgent and important tasks: projects to be completed immediately
- Not urgent, but important tasks: projects to be scheduled
- Urgent, but not important tasks: projects to be delegated to

Iteration Task Board Example

To Do	Doing		Done
Tasks	Task Queue	Work-in-Progress (WIP)	Task Complete

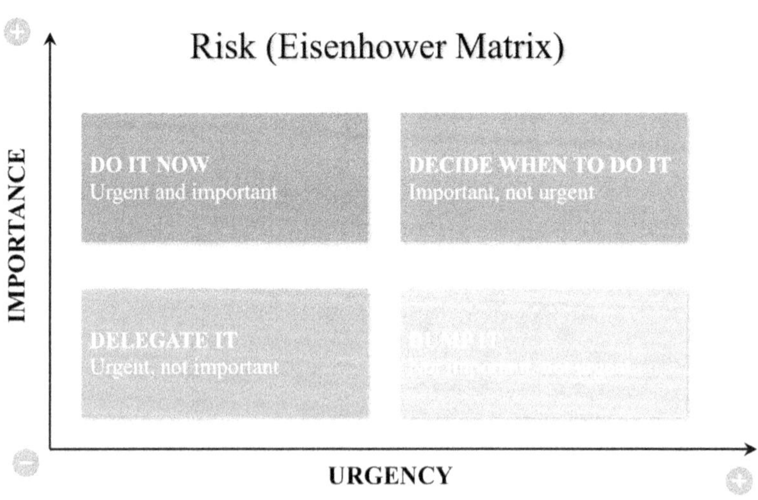

someone else
- Not urgent and not important tasks: projects to be deleted

Preparation and Strategy

Once you've created your to-do list and organized your tasks using the Eisenhower Matrix, it's time to revisit strategy. You need a strategy taking care of the most important parts of your life and business, which may include such general management tasks as branding, marketing, finance, accounting, supply chain, sales, customer service, etc. We're going to look at the first three of these tasks in more detail to understand how the projects that make your urgent and important list should be those that create opportunities while minimizing problems and concerns.

Branding

A good brand tells an enticing story. It explains your why, underscores the guiding principles that drive your organization, and does the heavy lifting for you by living in your employees' and customers' hearts and souls.

To create a successful story for your brand, you need to:

- know who you are and what you stand for
- have a clear vision
- find your audience
- adapt your expertise to your audience
- write your story
- keep it simple
- stay human
- live your story on a daily basis
- never let anyone take your story away from you

Brands use storytelling for advertising purposes and to highlight their products, projects, or businesses. The goal of brand storytelling is to seduce the members of a target market by manipulating their emotions, rather than by selling the merits of a particular product or service.

The most successful business strategies combine brand storytelling with an effective marketing plan that connects with customers, so let's turn to marketing now.

Marketing

Your marketing strategy lays out how you will market your products, services, or business to your customers. It states your goals and how you are going to achieve them. There are so many ways you can market your business, but any strategy should include these basics at a minimum:

- analysis of market opportunities
- customer targeting
- offer positioning
- action plan (marketing mix)
- control and review

When creating your marketing strategy, keep in mind your goals. Do you want to generate sales in the next three weeks? Develop a ten-year growth plan? The strategy you create depends on the business goals you have defined. Some of them may be:

- increase sales
- attract new customers
- introduce a new product or service
- increase market share
- increase brand awareness
- improve customer loyalty

The more specific you can be in terms of what constitutes "success" in a particular goal—for example, increasing market share by 1%—the better your odds of achieving that goal through marketing.

Finance

Finance strategy aims to identify all available and potential resources, and put in place a plan to effectively utilize them toward the end of achieving your business goals. Finance strategy also ensures sufficient and regular funding for a project, which is critical when developing a new or existing business activity.

It can sometimes be difficult for an entrepreneur to implement their financial strategy if their business model is not yet well-defined. Most of the time, financial partners wait until the project is mature enough to invest in it.

This wait-and-see approach limits the risks for funders, but it forces many entrepreneurs to launch their projects without full financing. In this context, a successful financial strategy limits the risk to both parties by creating milestones and structuring the investment process.

Implementing Preparation

You can strategize all day long, but if you don't have the knowledge or tools to strategize effectively, you're wasting your time. Here are some steps to take when preparing to prepare.

Educate Yourself

No one's born knowing everything you need to run a business. Leadership, sales, negotiations, customer service, emotional intelligence, mindfulness—some of these skills may come easily to you, and some you may need additional training in.

Identify where you're lacking, and get help! Maybe you hire a coach to show you the way, or maybe you find a mentor with whom you can exchange ideas and from whom you can get a second opinion. Another great option is to join or create a business mastermind group. This small group of people is a safe and useful space for brainstorming new ideas or gathering tips and tricks from others who have been there.

Understand the Business Environment

Political, cultural, and religious factors can all influence the business environment. Take pains to familiarize yourself with those factors influencing your team and industry, allow for them in your strategy, and be ready to embrace any changes that might impact you.

Identify Requirements

One critical part of pre-planning/preparation is identifying all functional and technical requirements for your project, product, or service. These tools can help you capture them:

- questionnaires
- charter
- contracts (Note: There are a lot of different contract types)
- RFP (request for proposal), RFQ (request for quote)
- BRD (business requirement document—some companies may call it "product requirements")
- business case
- statement of work
- case studies
- research

Challenge Constraints

It's important for entrepreneurs especially to take stock of their own limitations. They generally make very quick decisions without considering every possibility. The reality is that every business or project comes with constraints—limiting factors like the size of the market, the nature of demand in the market, the availability of supply, the quality and skill of employees, etc. It's important to identify these barriers and accept them before making any irrational decisions. Doing so will help you understand what's holding you back, and give you a clearer vision of all the possible paths and their consequences.

Set Expectations

The nature of business requires being in constant communication with many people. Whether they're employees or customers, it's important to set expectations from day one if you want to succeed in your business. All parties need to be "on the same page" regarding the work that needs to be done and targets that need to be achieved as part of your overall business strategy."All parties" in this case means your stakeholders. Depending on your business type, any of the following may be considered stakeholders:

- investors
- shareholders
- customers (clients)
- employees
- suppliers
- contractors
- managers
- sponsors
- project managers
- product managers
- communities

Communication Plan

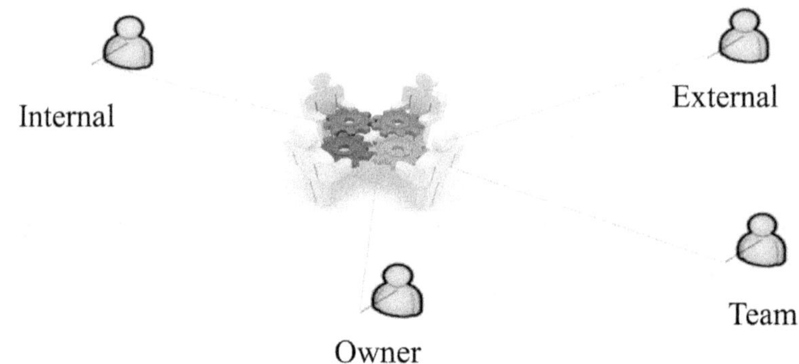

To effectively set clear expectations for your stakeholders, make sure you have a good communication plan in place. The communication plan refers to how information will be distributed to the team internally and to clients externally. It is always a good idea to sync-up internally before meeting with the client. We always say we don't want the customers to see our dirty laundry. The communication plan addresses the following concerns:

- who needs the project information
- what information will be communicated
- how the information will be communicated
- when the information will be distributed

Launch Meetings

Conduct your first meeting internally to identify internal and external project requirements and define what will be shared with customers. This "kickoff" meeting has the purpose of syncing up your team so everyone can hit the ground running.

The second meeting should be an external meeting for which you have already prepared and rehearsed what needs to be discussed and shared with customers.

Putting It All Together: Prepare to Avoid Negative Outcomes

Preparation/pre-planning is the most effective way to avoid negative outcomes. People who don't take the time to invest in preparation often find themselves overwhelmed dealing with the consequences. The COVID-19 pandemic is a clear example of how preparation could have limited the devastating damage visited

Communication Type (Meetings)	Objective of Communication	Frequency
Kickoff Meeting	Discuss the launch of the project with the team; review project objectives, requirements, timeline, and budget	Once
Project Team	Review status of the project with the team	Weekly
Technical Design	Discuss and develop technical design solutions for the project	As-needed
Monthly Project Status	Report on the status of the project to management	Monthly
Project Status Reports	Report activities, progress, costs, and issues	Monthly

upon people and businesses.

Preparation starts with anticipating and accepting all possible limitations and failures. While it's not always easy to imagine how failure might play out, it's surely the best way to identify potential pitfalls and choose the most suitable path. The FMEA Method (discussed in the next section) is one tool that can help you prepare efficiently.

Because the perception of what counts as "being prepared" varies from one person to another, it's important to ask yourself the right questions and think about how preparation could be useful to you in your business. If nothing else, the Eisenhower Matrix is fantastic for organizing your tasks according to importance and urgency and increasing your everyday effectiveness.

Once you understand the importance of preparation, use it to help you strategize critically, defining the path your business will take by prioritizing those projects that promise you the biggest benefits.

Finally, remember that you're not alone. An experienced mentor or coach can teach you what you don't know and help you to generate new ideas. Part of what they can brainstorm with you is the ins and outs of your business environment. The better you know the needs of and influences on your stakeholders, the easier it is to set goals, requirements, and expectations, while transforming constraints into business opportunities.

Part 2b Workbook:
Pre-Planning Tools

Practice Pre-mortems

A pre-mortem in business is the hypothetical opposite of a medical post-mortem. If a post-mortem determines cause of death, a pre-mortem is a thought exercise that asks participants to imagine a project has failed, then work backward to find out why. Pre-mortems are all about anticipation and setting expectations for the project team. You should believe that failure is probable and determine what it would look like before making any major decisions. With so many paths to choose from, pre-mortems can help you identify the best possible outcomes for your business.

In general, people tend to fear failure and are reluctant to consider the negative consequences of a chosen path. Perhaps a story about the cobra effect will demonstrate why pre-mortems are so important.

When the British were colonizing India, they were concerned with the number of venomous cobra snakes in Delhi. To solve the problem, they decided to offer a bounty for every dead cobra. This "solution" led to cobra breeding practices as a source of income. The government responded by canceling the reward, which resulted in even more cobras in Delhi after the breeders set them free.

Theoretically, the cobra effect could have been avoided altogether. If you force yourself to evaluate all the possible consequences, good and bad, of a particular decision, you will be more efficient in identifying and establishing which path is best for you.

Failure Mode and Effects Analysis

"I know you think you understand what you thought
I said but I'm not sure you realize that what you
heard is not what I meant."
—Unknown

FMEA stands for Failure Mode and Effects Analysis. It was developed by the American Army in the early 1940s and later used by NASA for the Apollo program. FMEA is a preventive method for identifying the points of failure likely to penalize performance,

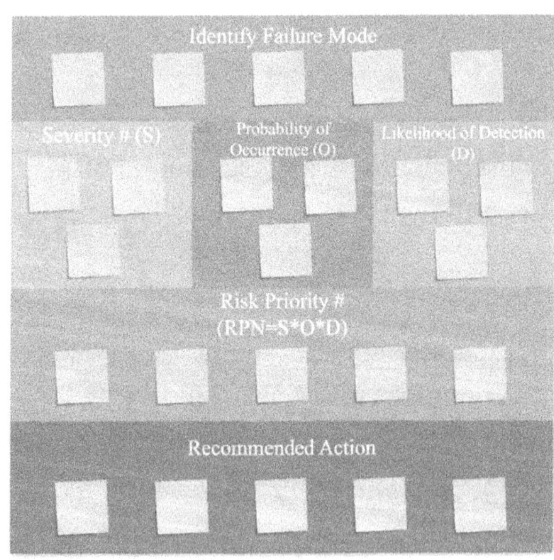

accomplished by listing and organizing foreseeable failure modes and their consequences during the implementation of a process or a product. It's therefore a valuable tool to ensure compliance with customer specifications and regulatory requirements.

PLAN

CHAPTER FIVE

Project Planning

*"It's better to sleep on what you plan to do than to
be kept awake by what you've done."*
—Unknown

There is nothing worse than spending time and resources on tasks that won't help achieve your goals. Once you're in the execution phase, there's no turning back. All your actions will have consequences, positive or negative. Only a solid plan will save your business from unexpected results.

Planning—the second P in the Three Ps approach—gives you control over choices and decisions rather than leaving things up to chance or giving others the opportunity to make decisions on your behalf. It's the next logical step in the project lifecycle after preparation/pre-planning because it involves deciding how to implement everything you learned in the preparation stage to get ready for the final stage, performance.

This chapter will provide the necessary methods and tools for planning your projects effectively.

Understanding Planning

Planning is putting in place a series of actions to achieve a goal or complete a project. For some, creating a plan may seem complex and overwhelming, but in reality, it can be as simple as answering the following questions:

- What kind of work will you be doing?
- Why will you be doing this work?
- How are you going to do the work?
- Who else will be doing the work?
- What resources will you need for the work?
- What will it cost to complete the work?
- Where is the location of the work?
- When will the work be done?

Think of the plan as a master contract that includes the most relevant project information, such as project description, timeline, budget, team, concerns, and much more.

Forms of Planning

Planning is an iterative and continuous process achieved through three basic steps:

1. Requirements: Define the work that needs to be done and the results that need to be achieved for the success of your project (see the Project Chart section in this chapter).
2. Schedule: Determine how much time is needed to complete the job in line with requirements in step 1.
3. Budget: Calculate the amount of time and money you're willing to spend on your project based on the estimated schedule in step 2.

A simple example of project planning is house renovation. You can easily find yourself exceeding the allocated budget if you don't carefully plan your renovation. By defining exactly what work needs done, how it will be done, who will do it, and when the work will be done by (completion time), you can develop a clearer vision of your project and, fingers crossed, avoid any bad surprises.

Because the most appropriate planning methods and tools will vary in accordance with the project scale, degree of complexity, and available resources, what's important is to adapt your planning to your project needs. Here are some components to consider when creating a project plan:

- goals and objectives
- deliverables (business and functional if applicable)
- milestones (schedule)
- budgets
- training
- team
- communication (tracking and sharing progress)
- metrics

After you've determined your project needs, try one or more of the following methods of planning.

Project Chart

The most popular project or business chart is the organizational chart. If you've ever looked at a directory of employees listed by rank or title, you're certainly familiar with it. Now, instead of listing people in your chart, list the tasks that need to be done on a project from start to completion. Not sure what tasks are relevant? You can generally find this information in the request for proposal (RFP), the contract, or the statement of work (SOW).

To build your project chart, invest in sticky notes and a poster board! These materials are affordable and easy-to-use, and can help you organize your ideas while increasing your productivity.

Work Structure Diagram

A work structure diagram breaks down all the work for a project into smaller pieces, so that you can more easily estimate your time, cost, etc. Because it's so versatile, this diagram could also be modified to include available resources, project requirements, associated activities, and other milestones. Using a work structure diagram makes your project more manageable and less overwhelming.

Below is an example of a work structure diagram for building a house. You can create the same for your startup.

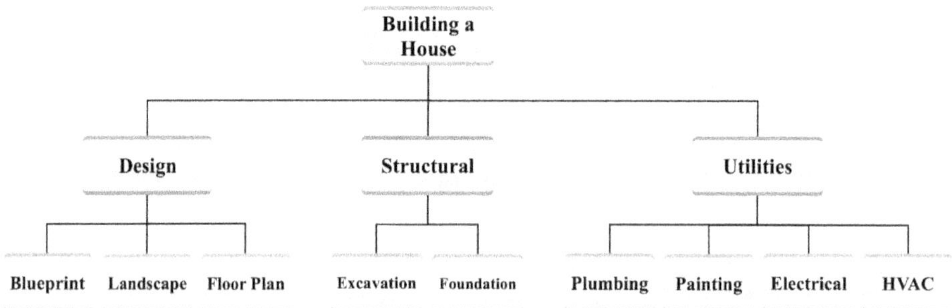

Work Structure Diagram

Planning and Strategy

The project chart and the work structure diagram are only useful so long as you are strategic about allocating resources properly and attempting to mitigate risks. Let's look at these now.

Resources

After breaking down your tasks, you need to define how they'll be completed and what resources they'll require. For each task, set clear expectations and determine who will be in charge of execution.

One resource to consider is people. Did you know that 14% of startups fail because of problems with their team?[1] You'll want to build a team you can trust, and train its members thoroughly to become fully operational.

Part of that training should involve thoughtful delegation. Delegating project tasks to your team can free you from minor responsibilities and allow you to concentrate on more critical and relevant concerns, such as customer relationships, sales targets, and competition. At the same time, delegation encourages team members to step up and into their own, preparing them to be leaders in their own right and thereby making your business more sustainable.

Money is another important project resource. Your budget represents the total estimated cost of completing a project during a certain period of time. It can include labor costs, procurement costs, operating costs, etc., and it's the tool that helps you control your spending as you progress in your project.

As opposed to the project chart, which is created using a top-down

---

1   https://www.cbinsights.com/research/startup-failure-reasons-top/

RESOURCES (TOOLS &
TERMINOLOGY)

approach, a budget is built using a bottom-up approach. You start with the specifics at the bottom of the hierarchy and progressively move up to the general.

Some important things to consider when defining your budget are:

- Cost estimates: Break down your project into tasks, activities, and milestones, and estimate the cost of each item on the task list.
- Contingency: What makes budgeting challenging is that you're working with estimates, not final figures, and there are almost always changes during the execution phase. It's important to set aside a contingency fund to handle them.
- Monitoring: Tracking is important in budgeting as well. You need to monitor your expenditures to ensure they're aligned with your planned budget.

Risks

Every project, situation, and event, no matter how well-planned, comes with inherent risks. These risks have an occurrence probability in the future that may negatively impact your project. They should therefore be addressed in the planning phase to prioritize requirements and identify the right resources and budgets.

Risk management is the process of identifying, assessing and controlling risks to a project's or organization's capital and earnings. In general, risk management looks like:

1. Planning
2. Assessing
3. Observing
4. Handling

Risks can be tricky to anticipate, however, and rarely is risk man-

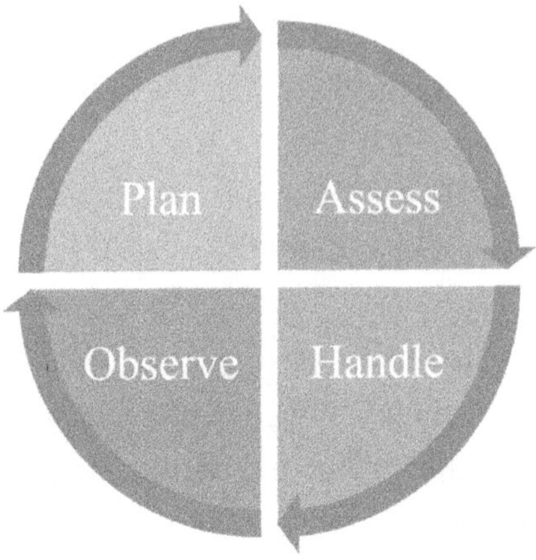

agement a one-and-done proposition. More often, it's a continuous process that must be revisited and revised regularly.

Putting It All Together: Implementing Planning

Planning is a proactive process that you undertake by answering some basic questions about your project and defining your requirements, schedule, and budget. Once you know these, you can map your project tasks into a project chart or work structure diagram, and delegate tasks to team members to increase overall productivity. Throughout the project, you'll want to keep tabs on your resources and budget, which is easier if you've already evaluated and built in accommodations for risks. Don't forget that risk management is ongoing. Having a plan in place will help you handle any negative consequences without impacting your progress or the completion date of your project.

CHAPTER SIX

Project Performance

The last P in the Three Ps approach, after pre-planning/preparation and planning, is performing. In this chapter, we'll focus on project performance and tracking any issues or concerns that may arise during the project. The goal is to stick as closely as possible to the original plan throughout the project's duration, including meeting your initial schedule and budget. It's a surefire way to achieve customer satisfaction.

Note: Continuous communication with all stakeholders is an essential part of performance. You will want to make sure that your team is meeting the project requirements on-schedule, and that your customer is being apprised of their progress. This phase is when you're most likely to spend the bulk of your money. Track all expenditures and schedule challenges that may cause delays or additional costs during execution, and be ready to take corrective actions to minimize the consequences.

Understanding Performance

Performance is another word for execution. In this phase, you put your plan into motion, keeping track of what's been accomplished

PERFORM

and work that has yet to be done. Your objective is to make sure
the final product is ready to be delivered to the customer on time.
Let's break down the steps that go into performance now.

Shipping

"Your job isn't to be creative. Your job is to ship."
—Seth Godin

To ship literally means to put the final product or service in the
hands of your customers. Shipping on schedule demonstrates that
you are committed to meeting the required specifications within
the agreed-upon budget.

Measurement

*"The first 90 percent of a project takes 90 percent
of the time; the last 10 percent takes the other 90
percent of the time."*
—Unknown

Metrics are performance measurements that you can use to track
the progress of your project and evaluate the results of your work.
Most works-in-progress will be measured by deliverables or milestones. Metrics only apply to those parts of your product or service
that actually meet customer requirements. For this reason, schedule and budget aren't metrics—only progress toward the finished
product or service is.

When determining what to measure, go ahead and exclude all incomplete tasks. Completion rates like "50%" or even "90%" just
create confusion, since such rates are more subjective and difficult
to measure.

Communication

Communication is important in both planning and execution. It ensures that the right information is shared with stakeholders, especially customers and employees. Throughout the project, issue status reports to share progress made on the project and monitor tasks, costs, risks, and time as compared to the project plan. You might try using a dashboard with three color codes—red, yellow, and green.

All communication and information-sharing should be precise and well-defined. To achieve this, limit the number of people involved in deciding what gets communicated and how. Here is the ultimate rule that founder Jeff Bezos implemented atAmazon to maximize effectiveness: "No meeting should be so large that two pizzas can't feed the whole group." The idea is that a larger group

Dashboard

Green	On time, on budget; good customer satisfaction
Yellow	Somewhat behind schedule, somewhat over budget; customer somewhat satisfied
Red	Behind schedule, over budget; customer is not satisfied

of people has a higher rate of social interaction, which tends to decrease meeting productivity and dilute the effectiveness of decision-making. Sometimes it's better to have just enough people to optimize communication during the meeting.

Performance and Strategy

While executing project tasks, you may encounter unforeseen circumstances that require you to think on your feet and strategically adapt. Maybe you need to conduct additional trainings for your team around a new skill or course-correct when progress gets derailed. Don't worry; because you prepared and planned in advance, you're naturally going to be more resilient. Take a deep breath. You've got this!

Team Training

Proper training can be critical to the success of your project. As the project manager, you need to be aware when your team needs additional training or education. There are many types of training that can be conducted at different stages of a project, such as internal and external training, on-the-job training, and on-demand training. If at any time you feel unsure, return to your project plan and check in on (monitor) the project's progress. You should be able to determine where the sticking points are and what training your team needs to be more productive.

Risks

Novelist Arnold Bennett states in his book *The Great Adventure* that any change, even a change for the better, is always accompanied by drawbacks and discomfort.

Risks are due to unknown or uncertain project factors, any of which can affect your project progress. Some of the most common issues necessitating project adjustments are missed requirements due to incomplete information from the customer or the end developer. Additional risks include poor planning, lack of accountability among team members, and inadequate deadlines. Should a team find itself working overtime to deal with the "drawbacks and discomfort" of a change midway through a project, performance consequences may include decreased morale or productivity.

Corrective Actions

As opposed to preventive actions, taken before there are deviations from the baseline, corrective actions are taken after there have been deviations from the baseline. Thanks to tracking, you should be able to detect and identify issues at any stage of your project. Corrective actions aim to re-align an off-track project with the initial plan. For instance, you'll take corrective actions to fix a bug or avoid delays in delivery. However, they shouldn't be used to justify changes in requirements, schedule, and costs.

Putting It All Together: Performance Is Adaptation!

Performance or execution is all about tracking all the changes to and deviations away from stated project goals, budgets, or schedules that may prevent you from delivering your final product to your customer.

Unfortunately, even with the most comprehensive preparation and planning, deviations happen. Good monitoring practices, including clear communication and information-sharing (via a status report) between the right stakeholders can help get you back on track. It's also a good idea to know your risks, be ready to face them, and train your team when necessary. Adapt to project changes by implementing a solid corrective plan.

Remember: A job is not complete until you ship the final product—hopefully on-time, within the agreed-upon budget, and having met the required specifications.

ACHIEVE RESULT

PART 3
THE OUTCOMES

Interpreting Project Results

OUTCOMES & LESSONS LEARNED

Outcome

CHAPTER SEVEN

Project Outcomes and Lessons Learned

After executing and completing your project, it's time to analyze the results and determine what went well and where there's room for improvement. Evaluating the outcomes is a necessary step in project management, as learning from past mistakes ensures that subsequent projects or phases are conducted more efficiently. Internalizing "lessons learned" can also help you challenge failure in general, so you can grow as a person and achieve your business goals.

Dream Big ...

The most successful startups have achieved success because they are fully invested in their goals. They work hard, have access to relevant information, and are quick to bring new products to market. Furthermore, they are innovative, creative, connected, competitive, and customer-driven. After facing down every challenge to come their way, they can feel proud: At long last, they have fulfilled their dream by completing their project.

Maybe you haven't achieved success yourself yet. Perhaps you envisioned your startup project a few months or years ago, and while you aspire to make that dream a reality, you're in the middle of the process, with a long road to walk. Devote yourself to your goals knowing that in the end, you'll only feel rewarded and accomplished when your project is complete and you're able to provide your customers with tangible products or services. Let thoughts of success—whatever that looks like to you—fuel your determination to advance.

... But Accept Failure, Too

"Ever tried. Ever failed. No matter. Try again. Fail again. Fail better."
—Samuel Beckett

"If you never failed, you never tried anything new."
—Unknown

We all know what failure is. When you don't achieve the goal you set, you feel sad, ashamed, and discouraged. You might become convinced that trying isn't worth the pain of failing. But pain is just information. You can leverage it to come back stronger. Every time you try—and fail—is another opportunity to learn, evolve, and do better the next time.

Resiliency is the practice of making the best out of failure. Current research shows that courage and perseverance in the face of failure—i.e., resiliency—are as predictive of success as factors like intelligence. Those who succeed are those who are also the most determined. In other words, the only way to really fail is not to try.

High-level athletes know resiliency intimately, since they must fail *a lot* before finally winning their medal. A study conducted on ten Olympic gold medal winners revealed that repeated failure—due to poor performance, bad injuries, or family member losses—actually indirectly contributed to the subjects' eventual victory, when they used that pain to fuel their next attempt.

As Nkemdilim Begho of Future Software Resources Limited reminds us, "Failure is necessary for any learning curve." If we let it, failure can make us stronger, bolder, and less scared of taking risks.

Lessons Learned

Gleaning "lessons learned" is the process of reviewing previous experiences, isolating takeaways both positive and negative, and utilizing the gained knowledge to avoid repeating the same mistakes and improve future projects or stages.

To identify your own "lessons learned," follow these steps:

1. Prepare and share specific questions about the project. Give team members enough time to think about them individually before asking for their responses. Conduct a Lessons Learned meeting, and objectively discuss the team's responses.
2. Record the Lessons Learned meeting and send a report (see report template below) to the project team.

Whether your project outcomes are positive or negative, you have to identify them, accept them, and learn from them if you want to avoid them in the future. Even if your project was completed, you still need to take the time to evaluate what went wrong or what could be improved and share this information with your team. If your project was not completed, trust that failure is the push that will give you the determination to come back as a winner.

Lessons Learned Report
Project Name:
Project Sponsor:
Date:

1. Did the project meet the requirements, timeline, quality, and cost goals?

2. What went right with this project?

3. What went wrong with this project?

4. What will you do differently on the next project based on your experience working on this project?

Additional comments: (What main lessons did your team learn from this project? What did you struggle with? Did you learn anything new?)

PART 4
THE TEAM

Your Project and Other People

THE TEAM (WHO)

CHAPTER EIGHT

The Team

"Coming together is the beginning. Keeping together is progress. Working together is success."
—Henry Ford

Although I have already underlined the importance of building a solid team, we have not yet covered how to do so. This chapter will look at how to hire the best people and partner with them to develop a sustainable business, plus methods for leading, motivating, and growing your team down the line.

Team Building

Because human interactions are very complex, the success of a chosen path is always filled with challenges. It's often quite difficult to align many people on the same goals and create a suitable working environment. Therefore, the leader's dedication and skills are essential for creating and developing a cohesive team.

Pick the Right People

When creating the team that will become the backbone of your business, each member should be chosen wisely both for his/her competency and business values. One of those values should be inclusivity, since team diversity may mean that people from different cultural backgrounds will be constantly interacting on a daily basis. You have to provide the best working environment to increase productivity and avoid any social issues that may affect your team's performance.

Jacinda Ardern, New Zealand's president, said that any economic growth accompanied by worsening social outcomes is not success, it is a failure. To reinforce a sense of community and create a cohesive team, it is an excellent practice to encourage charitable corporate giving and/or conduct volunteer work with your team members.

Build Trust

Maya Hu-Chan states in her book *Saving Face: How to Preserve Dignity and Build Trust* that in order for people to trust you as a team member, you have to be fully engaged, influential, and 100% committed to the team's mission. You have to care about your teammates and consistently prove that you value them as people and professionals by respecting their dignity, pride, and self-esteem.

This is what Hu-Chan calls "saving face.""Why is face so important?" she asks. "Face represents one's self-esteem, reputation, status, and dignity. Face is social currency." She also adds,"Saving face requires having the other person's best interest in mind, understanding their perspective, and delivering constructive feedback." In that sense, saving face is less about the leader's ego, and more about how s/he can serve the team.

Another way to build trust is by doing what former Zappos CEO Tony Hsieh did. Rather than remain locked in the ivory tower of

PEOPLE

the CEO and removed from his employees' everyday experiences, he went to work in the call center alongside them. He found that even in today's demanding environment, most employees are friendly, work hard, and have a lot of fun. They make coffee, take out the trash, and bring their pets to work. By interacting with employees and encouraging them to make the workplace their own, Hsieh earned their trust, which then empowered his team to want to do their jobs well and take care of Zappos's customers.

Increase Motivation

Drive is what makes a team want to achieve business goals. There is nothing worse than an unmotivated team with no purpose or determination to help make the business succeed.

As a leader, you are responsible for maintaining a positive environment. You must supply the rationales that give your team's work meaning, and support them psychologically on their own success journeys. Below is an example of how Google provides to its employees the best working environment by focusing on five positive team characteristics:

1. Psychological safety: Team members feel safe taking risks and can be vulnerable in front of each other in their work environment
2. Dependability: Team members rely on each other to get their work done
3. Structure and clarity: Each team member has a clear role and responsibilities
4. Meaning: The assigned work feels personally important to team members
5. Impact: Team members think their work matters and they want to be the change

Team-building activities outside the office can also increase moti-

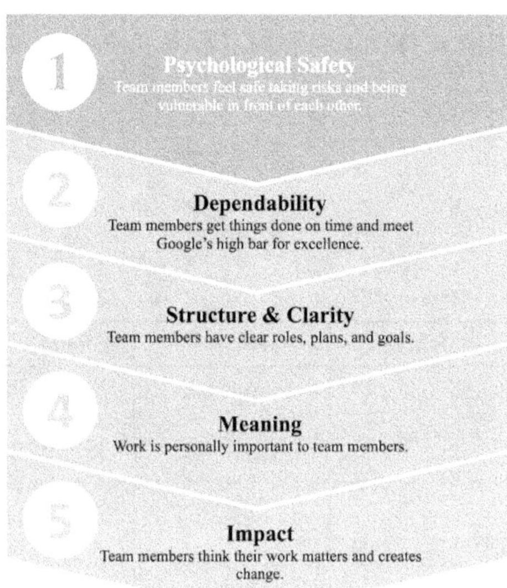

vation and foster teamwork. Water-tubing, golf, and volunteering are all fun, offsite activities that can motivate your team to develop their strengths and collaborate on common goals. Whatever the activity, it should encourage team members to work together rather than against one another.

Grow as a Team

Bruce Tuckman, an educational psychologist, identified a five-stage development process that most teams need to follow to become high-performing. He called these stages: forming, storming, norming, performing, and adjourning.

The most challenging phase is the storming stage, when conflicts are most likely to arise and when your team development risks hitting rock bottom. It's important to handle this stage carefully

Tuckman's Phases of Team Development

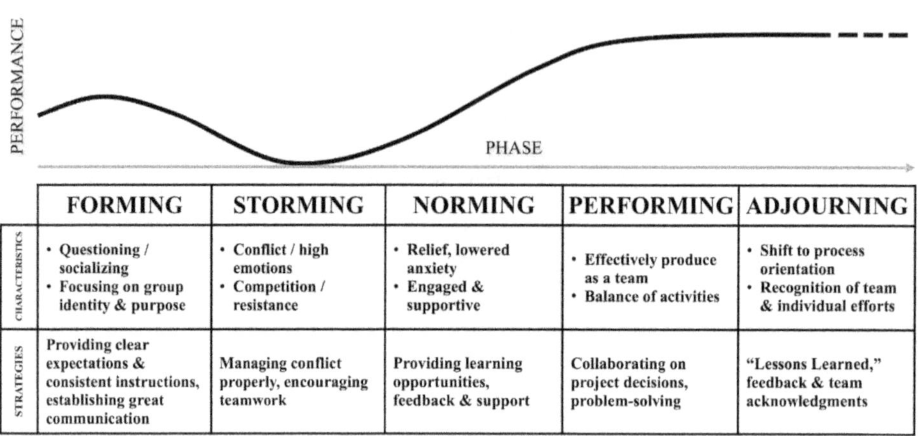

	FORMING	STORMING	NORMING	PERFORMING	ADJOURNING
CHARACTERISTICS	• Questioning / socializing • Focusing on group identity & purpose	• Conflict / high emotions • Competition / resistance	• Relief, lowered anxiety • Engaged & supportive	• Effectively produce as a team • Balance of activities	• Shift to process orientation • Recognition of team & individual efforts
STRATEGIES	Providing clear expectations & consistent instructions, establishing great communication	Managing conflict properly, encouraging teamwork	Providing learning opportunities, feedback & support	Collaborating on project decisions, problem-solving	"Lessons Learned," feedback & team acknowledgments

as overcoming it is the only way to bring your team together and increase, then stabilize, performance.

Teamwork Basics

According to Jon R. Katzenbach, author of *The Wisdom of Teams: Creating the High-Performance Organization*, "A team is a small group of people with complementary skills who are committed to a common purpose, performance goals, and approach for which they hold themselves mutually accountable."

A team will only be unified in their purpose, goals, and approach if all members can collaborate effectively in a favorable working environment. Some social norms that create a favorable working environment include:

- happiness and fun at the office
- honesty
- trust
- emotional intelligence
- mindfulness

Goals

The team's overarching goal should be to help you meet your project goals and make your business successful. Any team member who prevents you from achieving your goals is not a true part of the team and needs to be let go of immediately.

At the same time, keep in mind that you have a team for a reason. You can't do all the work by yourself. You need a team to help you work more effectively and handle different tasks and responsibilities. Author Israelmore Ayivor was right when he said, "Teamwork is the best ever investment. If I make 3 and you make 5, together we will not make 8. We will make 15. Leaders build active teams."

For that reason, it's your responsibility as the leader to communicate your goals to your team. A team can't move in the right direction without a map. Show them how serious and devoted you are to making the business or project successful. As President Theodore Roosevelt said, "People don't care how much you know, until they know how much you care."

Ethics

Ethics are moral principles, much like values, that dictate behavior inside and outside of the workplace. The four ethics I think should govern every team are respectfulness, fearless confrontation, civility, and seriousness.

Respectfulness: It's the art of being courteous, polite, decorous, civil, and deferential. The leader's job is to model respectfulness to all stakeholders at all times. You can do this by managing expectations, giving demonstrations, making connections, leading with your best self, and exhibiting good manners. When your teammates, business collaborators, users, etc. feel respected, they're more likely to show you respect in return.

Fearless confrontation: An experienced confrontationist knows how to skillfully diffuse situations in which people oppose or challenge each other. He can calm the situation and get people to agree and move forward. A confrontationist is not afraid of disagreement, and more importantly, can manage disagreement by conducting healthy debates, helping team members to hammer out their differences, and achieving superior results. Negotiating, managing trade-offs, solving solvable disagreements, managing unsolvable disagreements, and dealing with toxic people are all part of practicing fearless confrontation.

A civil person is one of morally good behavior or character. Civility means honoring the Golden Rule, or the idea that you should treat your teammates as you would like them to treat you. Being civil is hard work, particularly when ethical dilemmas crop up. When they do, you'll want to try advocating for honor, creating a shared team meaning, being all-in for the team, practicing appreciation, and maintaining objectivity.

Seriousness means that you have a strong desire to produce a high-quality product or offer a high-quality service. It conveys confidence, as you strive to show deep caring and sincerity about the project, program, ecosystem, and/or your team. Practicing progression and speed, reducing decision latency, and participating in retrospectives are all part of demonstrating seriousness.

Leadership

"Leadership is the art of getting others to want to do something that you believe should be done."
—Vance Packard

I've already said it, but I'll say it again: As a leader, you should set an example for your team and show them you know what you're doing and where your project is going. They should feel safe and confident working with you and following the path you've created, something that's only possible if you have the three skill subsets necessary to drive your project toward success. These subsets are soft skills, technical skills, and project management skills.

- Soft skills: personality traits, communication skills, social intelligence, and emotional intelligence that help you navigate your work environment
- Technical skills: a set of technical abilities that helps you perform practical tasks thanks to training and education
- Project management skills: skills (like the ones you're gaining from this book!) needed to see a project from start to finish while meeting the project requirements, budget, and schedule

If you have or develop these skills and you strongly believe in your goals, you can influence your team to believe in them as well. Your role as a leader is to inspire them to do their best for your business, which is only possible if you're coaching and mentoring them and making sure your team is cohesive, that no one feels unmotivated or excluded.

For that, you need to be the best version of yourself. Start by improving your own communication, health, and mindset. Consider taking an improvisation or public speaking class, and prioritizing your health and wellness through exercise, meditation, or sports.

**Project
Management Skills**

THRIVE

Soft Skills

**Technical
Skills**

Putting It All Together: The Perfect Team

One of your main objectives as an entrepreneur and a leader is to create the perfect team—a difficult task given how complex social interactions can be. With the right methods and tools, however, you can become a great leader, one who grows a great team. Start by working on yourself and improving your health, mindset, and skills. Before you know it, you'll start to inspire and lead your team toward your goals.

Along the way, remember to foster team building by encouraging activities that promote trust and increase motivation. Modeling strong ethics will create a safe and effective work environment, and help your team overcome any challenges that may arise.

Part 4 Workbook:
The Five Behaviors

The Five Behaviors approach combines the framework of team manager Patrick Lencioni's model for teamwork with personalized insights. It aims to create powerful, customized, and authentic team development solutions that empower individuals to make lasting change.

Based on Lencioni's book *The Five Dysfunctions of a Team*, the Five Behaviors approach emphasizes that to be successful in your project, you need to cultivate a team that understands, values, and practices these five key behaviors:

1. Results: focus on achieving collective results
2. Accountability: hold one another accountable
3. Commitment: commit to decisions
4. Conflict: engage in conflict constructively
5. Trust: trust one another

Implement these five behaviors, and you'll end up with a high-performing team for your startup.

Result
Accountability
Commitment
Conflict
Trust

CONCLUSION

Achieving Project Success

"Be the change you want to see in the world."
—Mahatma Gandhi

All the way back in Chapter One, I let Joseph M. Juran, The Total Quality Management (TQM) guru, give us the simplest definition of a project: "a problem scheduled for a solution." I added to that definition, "an opportunity scheduled for realization." In it most basic sense, a startup project is an opportunity to create meaning for a community. Projects not only add value to businesses through the production of an innovative product or service, but when those products and services are reliable and cost-effective, they also serve the customer and his community. Project success, therefore, is the result of efficiency, effectiveness, and quickness at bringing new products or services to market.

For any project to be successful, it is critical to first identify, then implement, your startup's vision, mission, goals, and guiding principles. Each one plays a vital role and should not be confused. The vision represents the aspirational and inspirational long-term goal of your business. The mission is the method by which day-to-day operations will fulfill the vision. Goals comprise the tangible to-

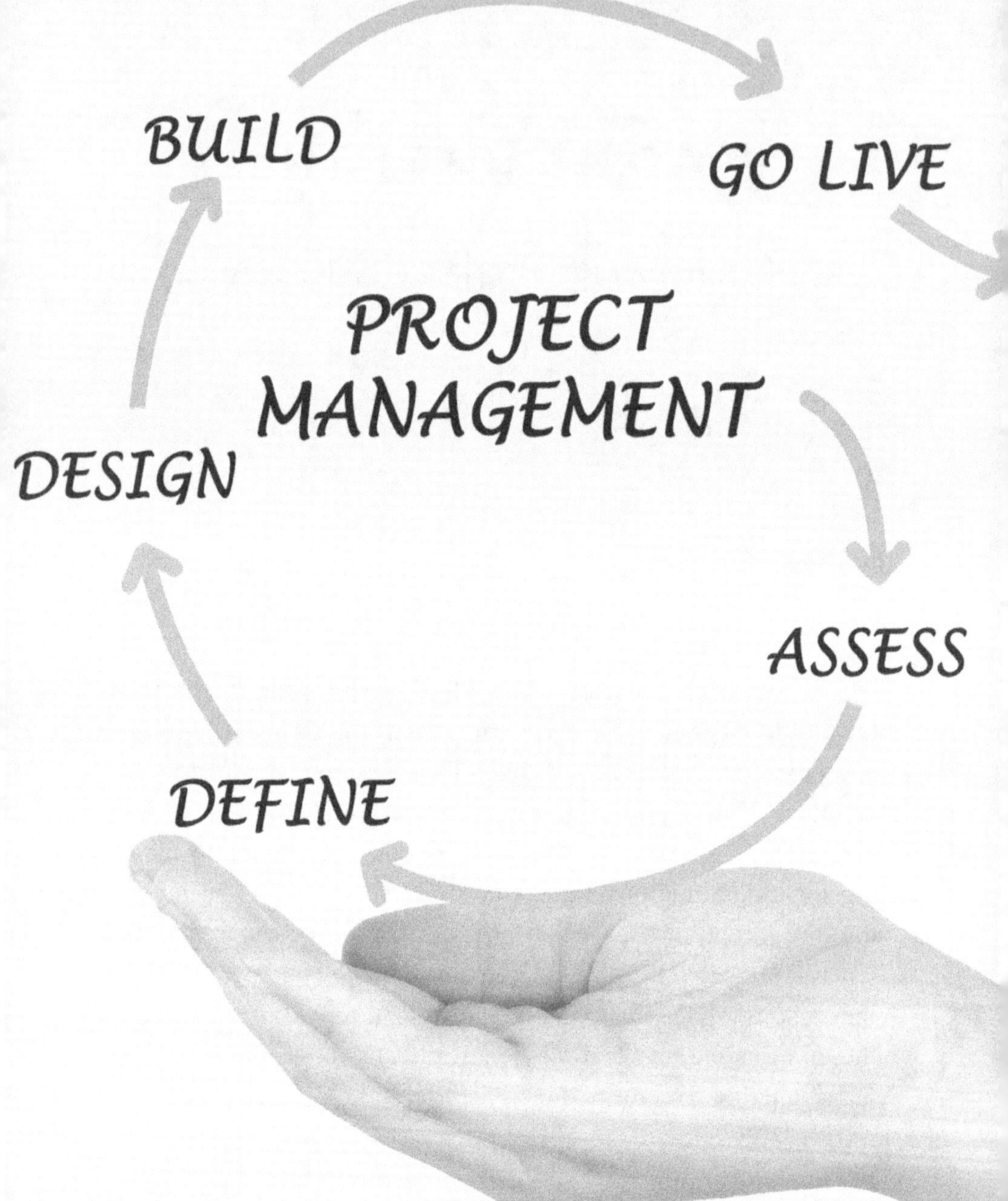

BUILD

GO LIVE

PROJECT
MANAGEMENT

DESIGN

ASSESS

DEFINE

do list necessary to achieve the vision and mission. Guiding principles are a set of non-negotiable morals and timeless values that inform business governance and set expectations about business conduct and decision-making. Together, these four elements guide your business like the North Star. They will steer you down the right path, where you will find your passion and purpose.

From your business goals comes the backbone of your strategy. To achieve your goals, you will need to take a set of clear, tangible, and specific measures. For example, if I am serious about giving fifty paid speaking engagements in the current fiscal year, then I must complete a number of actions to make that happen. In contrast to wishful thinking, strategy is all about action. Talking or dreaming about a goal won't get it done. As author Rick Page says, "Hope is not a strategy." Instead, you need a game plan, one in alignment with your business's vision, mission, and guiding principles. Once that's in place, you are ready to embark on your business journey.

My advice is to start working with the end in mind. When you settle on a product or service for your business, you should conceptualize its end state, then use the 3Ps (Prepare, Plan, and Perform) to figure out how to get there. Let's say you want to launch a startup in logistics and provide shipping and receiving services for your small community. What is the end game? Is the purpose to speed up deliveries? Or is it to give access to a distribution center to support the community that's experiencing delays in shipping and receiving merchandise?

Practicing the first P—preparation—will set up your project for maximum success by helping you to avoid negative outcomes. You can spend time and effort dealing with the consequences of a problem, or you can preempt said problem from the beginning by identifying and accepting your project's limitations and possible failures using the FMEA method. Start by asking yourself the hard questions and defining what tools and methods you can use to prepare your business to weather any storm. Educate yourself, do your research, and understand your business environment. Don't forget that having the right team onboard to manage your minor responsibilities can ensure you have enough time to concentrate on more critical tasks, like defining your business goals, setting expectations, and navigating business constraints.

After preparation comes the second P, planning. Clear requirements, a realistic schedule, and a workable budget are the key components of any successful plan, which you can create using a project chart or work structure diagram. The project chart is better suited to simpler projects and plans, while the work structure diagram can accommodate more complex project requirements. The latter is perfect for increasing productivity by breaking down a project plan into smaller tasks according to schedule, budget, and owner. As your team is one of your resources, be sure to delegate well.

When you're ready to perform your plan—the third P—remember that this stage, too, is interactive. You can't just put your project into motion then step back and watch it all happen; you have to monitor and track any changes or issues that may impact the progress of your project's milestones or deliverables. To ensure that you're delivering the best product to your customers with respect to planned requirements, budget, and schedule, use a status report to track and communicate your project status effectively. Take corrective actions promptly to mitigate any deviations from the initial plan.

At the end of the day, you'll have to face your outcomes. Whether positive or negative, they're an essential part of the process, and if you let them, they can be a great learning experience and a stepping stone to future success. Should your project fail, embrace the failure and use it as a reference point to improve your next project.

Should your project succeed, you can still evaluate how well the project was conducted and apply that information toward future projects. Use the Lessons Learned Report to document the experience and prepare for the next steps.

No matter what happens, know you're not alone. You have a team you've carefully cultivated that's rooted in trust and shared ethics, and you can and should process project results with them. They work hard for you, so be sure to motivate, inspire, and model for them how to be their best every day. Ultimately, your success will be defined by how productive your team is and how well you help each other prepare for, plan, and perform projects.

ABOUT THE AUTHOR

Ahmed Zouhair, DBA, PMP

Fluent in three languages (Arabic, French, and English) and with three degrees—including a doctorate in Business Administration—serial entrepreneur and seasoned project, product, and program management consultant Ahmed Zouhair knows the value of hard work. He also understands what it takes to build an empire from scratch. While today his international roster of clients includes companies and individuals from the education, IT, telecommunications, digital security, oil and gas, finance and banking, and non-profit sectors, Ahmed's career didn't start out that way. His first job after college involved collecting mud samples during 12-hour shifts on an oil and gas rig. Such tedious work in a harsh environment taught him patience and how to think on his feet when things go wrong. He likewise learned to interact with many different types of people, skills he would later refine as a volunteer business coach and workshop presenter for SCORE.

www.demystifyingprojectmanagement.com